TABLE OF CONTENT

ISBNS - International Standard Book Numbers
A Desktop Resource For Self-Publishing Authors
©Copyright 2013 by Dr. Leland Benton

DISCLAIMER AND TERMS OF USE AGREEMENT:

(Please Read This Before Using This Book)

This information is for educational and informational purposes only. The content is not intended to be a substitute for any professional advice, diagnosis, or treatment.

The author and publisher of this book and the accompanying materials have used their best efforts in preparing this book.

The author and publisher make no representation or warranties with respect to the accuracy, applicability, fitness, or completeness of the contents of this book. The information contained in this book is strictly for educational purposes. Therefore, if you wish to apply ideas contained in this book, you are taking full responsibility for your actions.

The author and publisher disclaim any warranties (express or implied), merchantability, or fitness for any particular purpose. The author and publisher shall in no event be held liable to any party for any direct, indirect, punitive, special, incidental or other consequential damages arising directly or indirectly from any use of this material, which is provided "as is", and without warranties. As always, the advice of a competent legal, tax, accounting, medical or other professional should be sought where applicable.

The author and publisher do not warrant the performance, effectiveness or applicability of any sites listed or linked to in this book. All links are for information purposes only and are not warranted for content, accuracy or any other implied or explicit purpose. No part of this may be copied, or changed in any format, or used in any way other than what is outlined within this course under any circumstances. Violators will be prosecuted.

Introduction – Everybody has heard about ISBNs; nobody knows about them!

Vita sine libris mors est - *Life without books is death*

ISBN 978-0-7334-2609-4

9780733426094

ISBNS - International Standard Book Numbers: A Desktop Resource For Self-Publishing Authors is an author's resource about a subject they hear about all of the time and that publishing platforms require but most authors really don't know anything about ISBNs.

I have 10-years of college and five degrees. People expect me to know things that I simply don't know and sometimes don't want to know. I sincerely could have done without the knowledge of colonics and what a "Brazilian" is when the girls in my office began gabbing about these two subjects. I always thought a Brazilian was a tiny little dude from Rio de Janero...no it's not...go with me on this one. I'm still trying to figure out the lyrics to the 60s song "Louie Louie" and I have no idea where flies sleep at night (lol). So much for 10-years of college!

Here's my point: there are some things we encounter daily that we know little about but use these things daily too. Furthermore, we also use words in our speech and writing that we don't REALLY know what they mean or have a very slight understanding to their meaning. ISBNs are one such subject.

When I woke up to this realization, I decided to publish desktop compendiums where readers could access information quickly and learn things that they needed to know.

My first compendium was titled "Latin Phrases."

http://www.amazon.com/dp/B006ITY7TW
https://www.createspace.com/4109722

I was amazed at how often we use Latin phrases in the English language but even more amazed how many of these phrases the users didn't know the meaning of but used them anyway. Phrases like "carpe diem (seize the day), non-sequitar (it does not follow), or quid pro quo (this for that). To add some zest to my Latin Phrases book, I even included some funny Latin phrases:

Volo anaticulam cumminosam meam! - *I want my rubber ducky!*

Visne saltare? Viam Latam Fungosam scio - *Do you want to dance? I know the Funky Broadway.*

Veni, Vidi, volo in domum redire - *I came, I saw, I want to go home.*

Vale, lacerte! - *See you later, alligator!*

Vah! Denuone Latine loquebar? Me ineptum. Interdum modo elabitur - *Oh! Was I speaking Latin again? Silly me. Sometimes it just sort of slips out.*

Tum podem extulit horridulum - *You are talking crap.*

Since I wrote Latin Phrases I have introduced three other "phrase" compendium books:

Investment Phrases

http://www.amazon.com/dp/B008LO3Y00

Legal Phrases
http://www.amazon.com/dp/B008LOA0Q6

Real Estate Phrases
http://www.amazon.com/dp/B008LQ7BMK

ISBNS - International Standard Book Numbers: A Desktop Resource For Self-Publishing Authors is the fifth book in this series and teaches a subject that all authors should know about in detail.

This book also addresses where authors can get ISBNs. The prices are all over the board and I have provided resources where you can acquire them reasonably.

Okay, let's continue with the lesson…

Chapter 1 – A Wikipedia Definition of ISBNs

I use Wikipedia often and I cannot provide a better explanation of ISBNs than what they have provided so I am using their definition and explanation. The original article can be found at the following URL:

http://en.wikipedia.org/wiki/International_Standard_Book_Number

The International Standard Book Number (ISBN) is a unique numeric commercial book identifier based upon the 9-digit Standard Book Numbering (SBN) code created by Gordon Foster, Emeritus Professor of Statistics at Trinity College, Dublin for the booksellers and stationers W. H. Smith and others in 1965.

The 10-digit ISBN format was developed by the International Organization for Standardization (ISO) and was published in 1970 as international standard ISO 2108   (However, the 9-digit SBN code was used in the United Kingdom until 1974.)

An SBN may be converted to an ISBN by prepending the digit '0'. Currently, the ISO TC 46/SC 9 is responsible for the ISBN. The ISO on-line facility only refers back to 1978.

Since 1 January 2007, ISBNs have contained 13 digits, a format that is compatible with Bookland EAN-13s.

Occasionally, a book may appear without a printed ISBN if it is printed privately or the author does not follow the usual ISBN procedure; however, this can be rectified later.

A similar numeric identifier, the International Standard Serial Number (ISSN), identifies periodical publications such as magazines.

Overview

An ISBN is assigned to **each edition and variation** (except reprintings) of a book, for example an ebook, a paperback, and a hardcover would each have a different ISBN. The ISBN is 13 digits long if assigned after January 1, 2007, and 10 digits long if assigned before 2007. An International Standard Book Number consists of 4 or 5 parts:

The parts of a 10-digit ISBN and the corresponding EAN-13 and barcode. Note the different check digits in each. The part of the EAN-13 labeled "EAN" is the Bookland country code.

1. for a 13-digit ISBN, a GS1 *prefix*: 978 or 979 (indicating the industry; in this case, 978 denotes book publishing)
2. the *group identifier*, (language-sharing country group)
3. the *publisher code*
4. the *item number* (title of the book), and
5. a checksum *character* or check digit.

The ISBN separates its parts (*group*, *publisher*, *title* and *check digit*) with either a hyphen or a space. Other than the check digit, no part of the ISBN has a fixed number of digits.

ISBN issuance

International Standard Book Numbers issuance is country-specific, and is tailored for each country's national goals. In Canada the stated purpose of issuing International Standard Book Numbers for no cost was to encourage Canadian culture. In the United Kingdom, United States, and other countries, the issuing of International Standard Book Numbers has become a profit center for the companies involved.

Australia: In Australia ISBNs are issued by the commercial library services agency Thorpe-Bowker and prices range from $40 for a single ISBN (plus a $55 registration fee for new publishers) through to $2,750 for a block of 1,000 ISBNs.

Canada: In Canada Library and Archives Canada, a government agency is the responsible entity, and there is no cost.

India: In India, Raja Rammohan National Agency for ISBN is responsible for registration of Indian Publishers, Authors, Universities, Institutions and Government Departments who are responsible for publishing books.

United Kingdom and Ireland: In the United Kingdom and Ireland the privately held company, Nielsen Book Services, part of Nielsen Holdings N.V., is the responsible entity, and there is a charge. ISBNs are sold in lots of ten or more.

United States: In the United States the privately held company R. R. Bowker is the responsible entity, and there is a charge, which varies depending upon the number of ISBNs purchased, with prices ranging from $125.00 for a single number.

Publishers and authors in other countries need to obtain ISBNs from their local ISBN Agency. A directory of ISBN Agencies is available on the International ISBN Agency website.

Group identifier

The group identifier is a 1 to 5 digit number. The single digit group identifiers are: 0 or 1 for English-speaking countries; 2 for French-speaking countries; 3 for German-speaking countries; 4 for Japan; 5 for Russian-speaking countries, 7 for People's Republic of China. An example 5 digit group identifier is 99936, for Bhutan. The allocated group IDs is: 0–5, 600–617, 7, 80–94, 950–989, 9927–9989, and 99901–99967. Some catalogs include books that were published with no ISBN but add a non-standard number with an as-yet unallocated 5-digit group such as 99985; this practice is not part of the standard. Books published in rare languages typically have longer group identifiers.

The original standard book number (SBN) had no group identifier, but affixing a zero (0) as prefix to a 9-digit SBN creates a valid 10-digit ISBN. Group identifiers form a prefix code; compare with country calling codes.

Publisher code

The national ISBN agency assigns the publisher number (cf. the Category: ISBN agencies); the publisher selects the item number. Generally, a book publisher is not required to assign an ISBN, nor is it necessary for a book to display its number (except in China; see below). However, most book stores only handle ISBN-bearing merchandise.

A listing of all the 628,000 assigned publisher codes is published, and can be ordered in book form (€558, US$915.46). The web site of the ISBN agency does not offer any free method of looking up publisher codes. Partial lists have been compiled (from library catalogs) for the English-language groups: identifier 0 and identifier 1.

Publishers receive blocks of ISBNs, with larger blocks allotted to publishers expecting to need them; a small publisher may receive ISBNs of one or more digits for the group identifier code, several digits for the publisher, and a single digit for the individual items. Once that block of ISBNs is used, the publisher may receive another block of ISBNs, with a different publisher number. Consequently, a publisher may have different allotted publisher numbers. There also may be more than one group identifier used in a country. This might occur if a popular identifier has used up all of its numbers. The cited list of identifiers shows this has happened in China and in more than a dozen other countries.

By using variable block lengths, a large publisher has few digits allocated for the publisher number and many digits allocated for titles; likewise countries publishing much have few allocated digits for the group identifier, and many for the publishers and titles. Here are some sample ISBN-10 codes, illustrating block length variations.

ISBN	Country or area	Publisher
99921-58-10-7	Qatar	NCCAH, Doha
9971-5-0210-0	Singapore	World Scientific
960-425-059-0	Greece	Sigma Publications
80-902734-1-6	Czech Republic; Slovakia	Taita Publishers
85-359-0277-5	Brazil	Companhia das Letras
1-84356-028-3	English-speaking area	Simon Wallenberg Press
0-684-84328-5	English-speaking area	Scribner
0-8044-2957-X	English-speaking area	Frederick Ungar
0-85131-041-9	English-speaking area	J. A. Allen & Co.
0-943396-04-2	English-speaking area	Willmann–Bell

0-9752298-0-X   English-speaking area   KT Publishing

Pattern

English-language publisher codes follow a systematic pattern, which allows their length to be easily determined, as follows:

Item number length	0- group identifier			1- group identifier			Total
	From	To	Publishers	From	To	Publishers	
6 digits	0-00-xxxxxx-x	0-19-xxxxxx-x	20	1-00-xxxxxx-x	1-09-xxxxxx-x	10	30
5 digits	0-200-xxxxx-x	0-699-xxxxx-x	500	1-100-xxxxx-x	1-399-xxxxx-x	300	800
4 digits	0-7000-xxxx-x	0-8499-xxxx-x	1,500	1-4000-xxxx-x	1-5499-xxxx-x	1,500	3,000
3 digits	0-85000-xxx-x	0-89999-xxx-x	5,000	1-55000-xxx-x	1-86979-xxx-x	31,980	36,980
2 digits	0-900000-xx-x	0-949999-xx-x	50,000	1-869800-xx-x	1-998999-xx-x	129,200	179,200
1 digit	0-9500000-x-x	0-9999999-x-x	500,000	1-9990000-x-x	1-9999999-x-x	10,000	510,000
Total			557,020	Total		172,990	730,010

Check digits

14

A check digit is a form of redundancy check used for error detection, the decimal equivalent of a binary checksum. It consists of a single digit computed from the other digits in the message.

ISBN-10 check digit calculation

The 2001 edition of the official manual of the International ISBN Agency says that the ISBN-10 check digit – which is the last digit of the ten-digit ISBN – must range from 0 to 10 (the symbol X is used instead of 10) and must be such that the sum of all the ten digits, each multiplied by the integer weight, descending from 10 to 1, is a multiple of the number 11. Modular arithmetic is convenient for calculating the check digit using modulus 11. Each of the first nine digits of the ten-digit ISBN – excluding the check digit, itself – is multiplied by a number in a sequence from 10 to 2, and the remainder of the sum, with respect to 11, is computed. The resulting remainder, plus the check digit, must equal 11; therefore, the check digit is 11 minus the remainder of the sum of the products.

For example, the check digit for an ISBN-10 of 0-306-40615-? is calculated as follows:

$$s = (0 \times 10) + (3 \times 9) + (0 \times 8) + (6 \times 7) + (4 \times 6) + (0 \times 5) + (6 \times 4) + (1 \times 3) + (5 \times 2)$$
$$= 0 + 27 + 0 + 42 + 24 + 0 + 24 + 3 + 10$$
$$= 130 = 12 \times 11 - 2$$

Thus the check digit is 2, and the complete sequence is ISBN 0-306-40615-2.

Formally, the check digit calculation is:

$$(10x_1 + 9x_2 + 8x_3 + 7x_4 + 6x_5 + 5x_6 + 4x_7 + 3x_8 + 2x_9 + x_{10}) \mod 11 \equiv 0.$$

The value x_{10} required to satisfy this condition might be 10; if so, an 'X' should be used.

The two most common errors in handling an ISBN (e.g., typing or writing it) are an altered digit or the transposition of adjacent digits. The ISBN check digit method ensures that these two errors will always be detected. However, if the error occurs in the publishing house and goes undetected, the book will be issued with an invalid ISBN.

Alternative calculation

```php
//PHP
function is_isbn_10_valid($ISBN10){
   if(strlen($ISBN10) != 10)
      return false;

   $a = 0;
   for($i = 0; $i < 10; $i++){
      if ($ISBN10[$i] == "X"){
         $a += 10*intval(10-$i);
      } else {//running the loop
         $a += intval($ISBN10[$i]) * intval(10-$i);
      }
   }
   return ($a % 11 == 0);
}
```

```python
#Python
def is_isbn10(isbn10):
   if len(isbn10) != 10:
      return False
   r = sum((10 - i) * (int(x) if x != 'X' else 10) for i, x in enumerate(isbn10))
   return r % 11 == 0
```

```ruby
#Ruby
def is_valid?(isbn)
  (isbn.length == 10) && (isbn.split('').inject([10,0]){|a, c| i,s = a; [s+i*c.to_i,i-1]}.first%11==0)
end
```

ISBN-13 check digit calculation

The 2005 edition of the International ISBN Agency's official manual covering some ISBNs issued from January 2007, describes how the 13-digit ISBN check digit is calculated.

The calculation of an ISBN-13 check digit begins with the first 12 digits of the thirteen-digit ISBN (thus excluding the check digit itself). Each digit, from left to right, is alternately multiplied by 1 or 3, then those products are summed modulo 10 to give a value ranging from 0 to 9. Subtracted from 10, that leaves a result from 1 to 10. A zero (0) replaces a ten (10), so, in all cases, a single check digit results.

For example, the ISBN-13 check digit of 978-0-306-40615-? is calculated as follows:

s = 9×1 + 7×3 + 8×1 + 0×3 + 3×1 + 0×3 + 6×1 + 4×3 + 0×1 + 6×3 + 1×1 + 5×3
  = 9 + 21 + 8 + 0 + 3 + 0 + 6 + 12 + 0 + 18 + 1 + 15
  = 93
93 / 10 = 9 remainder 3
10 − 3 = 7

Thus, the check digit is 7, and the complete sequence is ISBN 978-0-306-40615-7.

Formally, the ISBN-13 check digit calculation is:

$$x_{13} = (10 - (x_1 + 3x_2 + x_3 + 3x_4 + \cdots + x_{11} + 3x_{12}) \bmod 10) \bmod$$

This check system – similar to the UPC check digit formula – does not catch all errors of adjacent digit transposition. Specifically, if the difference between two adjacent digits is 5, the check digit will not catch their transposition. For instance, the above example allows this situation with the 6 followed by a 1. The correct order contributes 3×6+1×1 = 19 to the sum; while, if the digits are transposed (1 followed by a 6), the contribution of those two digits will be 3×1+1×6 = 9. However, 19 and 9 are congruent modulo 10, and so produce the same, final result: both ISBNs will have a check digit of 7. The ISBN-10 formula uses the prime modulus 11 which avoids this blind spot, but requires more than the digits 0-9 to express the check digit.

Additionally, if the sum of the 2nd, 4th, 6th, 8th, 10th, and 12th digits is tripled then added to the remaining digits (1st, 3rd, 5th, 7th, 9th, 11th, and 13th), the total will always be divisible by 10 (i.e., end in 0).

```java
// Java
public static boolean isISBN13Valid(String isbn) {
    int check = 0;
    for (int i = 0; i < 12; i += 2) {
        check += Integer.valueOf(isbn.substring(i, i + 1));
    }
    for (int i = 1; i < 12; i += 2) {
        check += Integer.valueOf(isbn.substring(i, i + 1)) * 3;
    }
    check += Integer.valueOf(isbn.substring(12));
    return check % 10 == 0;
}
```

```javascript
//JavaScript
function isValidISBN13(ISBNumber) {
    var check, i;

    ISBNumber = ISBNumber.replace(/-\s/g,'');

    check = 0;
    for (i = 0; i < 13; i += 2) {
      check += +ISBNumber[i];
    }
    for (i = 1; i < 12; i += 2){
      check += 3 * +ISBNumber[i];
    }
    return check % 10 === 0;
}
```

```php
//PHP
function is_isbn_13_valid($n){
```

```php
    $check = 0;
    for ($i = 0; $i < 13; $i+=2) $check += substr($n, $i, 1);
    for ($i = 1; $i < 12; $i+=2) $check += 3 * substr($n, $i, 1);
    return $check % 10 == 0;
}
```

```ruby
# Ruby
def isbn_checksum(isbn_string)
  digits = isbn_string.split(//).map(&:to_i)
  transformed_digits = digits.each_with_index.map do |digit, digit_index|
    digit_index.modulo(2).zero? ? digit : digit*3
  end
  sum = transformed_digits.reduce(:+)
end

def is_valid_isbn13?(isbn13)
  checksum = isbn_checksum(isbn13)
  checksum.modulo(10).zero?
end

def isbn13_checksum_digit(isbn12)
  checksum = isbn_checksum(isbn12)
  10 - checksum.modulo(10)
end
```

```python
# Python
def is_valid_isbn13(isbn13):
    total = sum(int(num) * weight for num, weight in zip(isbn13, (1, 3) * 6))
    ck = (10 - total) % 10
    return ck == int(isbn13[-1])
```

```c
// C/C++
bool is_valid_isbn13(char digits[13])
{
    int i, check=0;
    for (i=0; i<13; i+=2)
        check += digits[i];
    for (i=1; i<12; i+=2)
        check += 3*digits[i];
    return check%10==0;
```

```
}
# Bourne-Again SHell
function is_valid_isbn13 () {
declare ISBN="${1//[^[:digit:]]}"
declare -i CheckDigit=0

  for i in $(seq 0 12); do
    CheckDigit+=$(((${ISBN:$i:1}*(1 + 2*(i % 2))))
  done
  return $((CheckDigit % 10))
}
```

Errors in usage

Publishers and libraries have varied policies about the use of the ISBN check digit. Publishers sometimes fail to check the correspondence of a book title and its ISBN before publishing it; that failure causes book identification problems for libraries, booksellers, and readers.

Most libraries and booksellers display the book record for an invalid ISBN issued by the publisher. The Library of Congress catalogue contains books published with invalid ISBNs, which it usually tags with the phrase "Cancelled ISBN".

However, book-ordering systems such as Amazon.com will not search for a book if an invalid ISBN is entered to its search engine.

EAN format used in barcodes and upgrading

Currently the barcodes on a book's back cover (or inside a mass-market paperback book's front cover) are EAN-13; they may have a separate barcode encoding five digits for the currency and the recommended retail price. The number "978", the Bookland "country code", is prefixed to the ISBN in the barcode data, and the check digit is recalculated according to the EAN13 formula (modulo 10, 1x and 3x weighting on alternate digits).

Partly because of an expected shortage in certain ISBN categories, the International Organization for Standardization (ISO) decided to migrate to a thirteen-digit ISBN (ISBN-13). The process began January 1, 2005 and was planned to conclude January 1, 2007.[25] As of 2011, all the 13-digit ISBNs begin with 978. As the 978 ISBN supply is exhausted, the 979 prefix will be introduced. This is expected to occur more rapidly outside the United States. Originally, 979 was the Musicland code for musical scores with an ISMN. However, ISMN codes will differ visually as they begin with an "M" letter; the bar code represents the "M" as a zero (0), and for checksum purposes it will count as a 3.

Publisher identification code numbers are unlikely to be the same in the 978 and 979 ISBNs; likewise, there is no guarantee that language area code numbers will be the same. Moreover, the ten-digit ISBN check digit generally is not the same as the thirteen-digit ISBN check digit. Because the EAN/UCC-13 is part of the Global Trade Item Number (GTIN) system (that includes the EAN/UCC-14, the UPC-12, and the EAN-8), it is expected that ISBN-generating software should accommodate fourteen-digit ISBNs.

Barcode format compatibility is maintained, because (aside from the group breaks) the ISBN-13 barcode format is identical to the EAN barcode format of existing ISBN-10s. So, migration to an EAN-based system allows booksellers the use of a single numbering system for both books and non-book products that is compatible with existing ISBN-based data, with only minimal changes to information technology systems. Hence, many booksellers (e.g., Barnes & Noble) migrated to EAN barcodes as early as March 2005. Although many American and Canadian booksellers were able to read EAN-13 barcodes before 2005, most general retailers could not read them. The upgrading of the UPC barcode system to full EAN-13, in 2005, eased migration to the ISBN-13 in North America.

See also

- ASIN (Amazon Standard Identification Number)
- CODEN (serial publication identifier currently used by libraries; replaced by the ISSN for new works)
- DOI (Digital Object Identifier)
- ESTC (English Short Title Catalogue)
- ETTN (Electronic Textbook Track Number)
- ISAN (International Standard Audiovisual Number)
- ISMN (International Standard Music Number)
- ISWC (International Standard Musical Work Code)
- ISRC (International Standard Recording Code)
- ISSN (International Standard Serial Number)
- ISWN (International Standard Wine Number)
- LCCN (Library of Congress Control Number)
- List of group-0 ISBN publisher codes
- List of group-1 ISBN publisher codes
- OCLC number (Online Computer Library Center number [2])
- Registration authority
- SICI (Serial Item and Contribution Identifier)
- Special: Booksources, Wikipedia's ISBN search page
- VD 16 (Verzeichnis der im deutschen Sprachbereich erschienenen Drucke des 16. Jahrhunderts)(in English: *Bibliography of Books Printed in the German Speaking Countries of the Sixteenth Century*)
- VD 17 (Verzeichnis der im deutschen Sprachraum erschienenen Drucke des 17. Jahrhunderts)(in English: *Bibliography of Books Printed in the German Speaking Countries of the Seventeenth Century*)

Chapter 2 – What's the Difference Between Cheap ISBNs & Expensive Ones?

I get asked the question, "What is the difference between cheap ISBNs and expensive one?" and there is a BIG DIFFERENCE!!!!!

When you purchase an ISBN from a cheap site, the site is more than likely a reseller of ISBNs. This means THEY are listed as the publisher and not YOU! What this further means is that you may only use the ISBN when you publish with them. It is not universal where you can use it anywhere.

But don't freak out on me just yet. You need to determine what you are going to use the ISBN for. For example, when I publish on CreateSpace or Smashwords, I always just get their free ISBN.

I only publish through 7-platforms because these platforms publish on all of the other major ones so there is no need to purchase a universal ISBN.

A universal ISBN costs for one single one about $125. This ISBN can be used anywhere you publish but in my webinar I give you the 7-platforms that are only worth publishing on so think this through before you go out and spend your hard earned money. (Go here for the recording: http://tinyurl.com/epubwebinar).

Here is what you look for in a site's FAQs:

If I purchase an ISBN from ePub Bud, how does it get officially assigned to my book?

There is a centralized database of ISBN information at bowkerlink.com, but it's not actually required to register any information there.

The main purpose of an ISBN is that it is unique... once you've got your ISBN(s), just go and use them! (If you're really worried, we do have a 100% unconditional money-back guarantee on them forever as well.)

Nevertheless, we can go ahead and register a book in the Bowker database for you; after you purchase your ISBN(s) there will be a link "Assign Book Info" you can click to register your book's info with Bowker's Books-In-Print database automatically from our site!

Note: all the ISBNs we distribute have "ePub Bud" as the publisher in the Bowker database. Don't worry though, that fact does not convey any rights to us, nor does it affect your ability to do anything you'd like with your book (or the ISBN), publish it anywhere, keep all royalties for yourself, etc, etc.. Bowker just won't let us change the publisher field for less than $75 an ISBN (and therefore we don't offer that)!

This is from ePubBud's site and they sell ISBNs for just $9

http://www.epubbud.com/help.php#isbn

So look before you leap and determine first what the goal is!!!

Chapter 3 – Frequently Asked Questions About ISBNs

http://www.isbn.org/standards/home/isbn/us/isbnqa.asp

Frequently Asked Questions about the ISBN

What is an ISBN?

The International Standard Book Number (ISBN) is a 10-digit number that uniquely identifies books and book-like products published internationally.

What is the purpose of an ISBN?

The purpose of the ISBN is to establish and identify one title or edition of a title from one specific publisher and is unique to that edition, allowing for more efficient marketing of products by booksellers, libraries, universities, wholesalers and distributors.

What is the format of the ISBN?

Every ISBN consists of ten digits and whenever it is printed it is preceded by the letters ISBN. The ten-digit number is divided into four parts of variable length, each part separated by a hyphen.

Does the ISBN have any meaning imbedded in the numbers?

The four parts of an ISBN are as follows:

Group or country identifier which identifies a national or geographic grouping of publishers;

Publisher identifier which identifies a particular publisher within a group;

Title identifier which identifies a particular title or edition of a title;

Check digit is the single digit at the end of the ISBN which validates the ISBN.

Why do some ISBNs end in an "X"?

In the case of the check digit, the last digit of the ISBN, the upper case X can appear. The method of determining the check digit for the ISBN is the modulus 11 with the weighting factors 10 to 1. The Roman numeral X is used in lieu of 10 where ten would occur as a check digit.

Who can assign ISBNs to a publisher?

There are over 160 ISBN Agencies worldwide, and each ISBN Agency is appointed as the exclusive agent responsible for assigning ISBNs to publishers residing in their country or geographic territory. The United States ISBN Agency is the only source authorized to assign ISBNs to publishers supplying an address in the United States, U.S. Virgin Islands, Guam and Puerto Rico and its database establishes the publisher of record associated with each prefix.

Once an ISBN publisher prefix and associated block of numbers has been assigned to a publisher by the ISBN Agency, the publisher can assign ISBNs to publications it holds publishing rights to. However, after the ISBN Agency assigns ISBNs to a publisher, that publisher cannot resell, re-assign, transfer, or split its list of ISBNs among other publishers. These guidelines have long been established to ensure the veracity, accuracy and continued utility of the international ISBN standard.

As defined by the ISO Standard, the ISBN publisher prefix (or "root" of the ISBN) identifies a single publisher. If a second publisher subsequently obtains an ISBN from the assigned publisher's block of ISBNs, there will be no change in the publisher of record for any ISBN in the block as originally assigned. Therefore, searches of industry databases for that re-assigned ISBN will identify the original owner of that assigned prefix as the publisher rather than the second publisher. Discovering this consequence too late can lead to extensive costs in applying for a new prefix, re-assigning a new ISBN, and potentially leading to the application of stickers to books already printed and in circulation.

If you are a new publisher, you should apply for your own ISBN publisher prefix and plan to identify and circulate your books properly in the industry supply chain. You may encounter offers from other sources to purchase single ISBNs at special offer prices; you should be wary of purchasing from these sources for the reasons noted above. There are unauthorized re-sellers of ISBNs and this activity is a violation of the ISBN standard and of industry practice. A publisher with one of these re-assigned ISBNs will not be correctly identified as the publisher of record in Books In Print or any of the industry databases such as Barnes and Noble or Amazon or those of wholesalers such as Ingram. If you have questions, contact the US ISBN Agency for further advice.

Who is eligible for an ISBN?

The ISBN Agency assigns ISBNs at the direct request of publishers, e-book publishers, audio cassette and video producers, software producers and museums and associations with publishing programs.

How long does it take to get an ISBN?

Allow 15 business days for non-priority processing from the time an ISBN application is received at the agency (not from the date sent by the publisher.) Priority processing is two business days from the time an application is received at the agency. Express processing is 24 business hours.

How much does it cost to get an ISBN?

There is a service fee to process all ISBN applications. Service fee information is contained on the application. Priority and Express processing involve an additional fee.

NOTE: The processing service charge is NON-REFUNDABLE.

What do I do when I receive the ISBN and where is it printed?

An ISBN should be assigned to each title or product, including any backlist or forthcoming titles. Each format or binding must have a separate ISBN (i.e. hardcover, paperbound, VHS video, laserdisc, e-book format, etc). A new ISBN is required for a revised edition. Once assigned, an ISBN can never be reused. An ISBN is printed on the lower portion of the back cover of a book above the bar code and on the copyright page.

How & where do I register my ISBN?

Once ISBNs have been assigned to products they should be reported to R.R. Bowker as the database of record for the ISBN Agency. Companies are eligible for a free listing in various directories such as Books in Print, Words on Cassette, The Software Encyclopedia, Bowker's Complete Video Directory, etc.

NOTE: Receiving just your ISBNs does **NOT** guarantee title listings. To ensure your titles get in the Books in

Print database **you must submit your title information.**

Book titles should be registered with Books in Print at **www.bowkerlink.com**

Can a publisher have both an ISBN & an ISSN?

Both numbering systems are used for books in a series and with annuals or biennials. The ISBN identifies the individual book in a series or a specific year for an annual or biennial. The ISSN identifies the ongoing series, or the ongoing annual or biennial serial. If a publication has both, each should be printed on the copyright page.

How can I find an assigned ISBN?

The Publications (hard copy listings) in which the assigned ISBNs appear are Publishers, Distributors & Wholesalers of the United States (http://www.bowker.com/catalog/000062.htm), published by R.R. Bowker, and Literary Market Place (http://www.literarymarketplace.com/) , published by Information Today.

How are ISBNs used in a Bar Code & how do I obtain one?

The ISBN can be translated into a worldwide compatible bar code format. Publishers who wish to have their ISBNs translated into worldwide compatible bar codes can now make their request directly online at www.isbn.org or www.bowkerbarcode.com . Bar code scanning is a required step required by for many retailers in the sales transaction process for book publications and book-related items. We hope that offering this service will save you time and enable you to meet all of your transaction partners' requirements.

How do I select the correct amount of ISBNs?

ISBNs are sold in blocks of 10, 100, and 1000. When purchasing ISBNs, we recommend that you estimate the amount of publications you will be publishing within the next five years, and select the block that best suits your needs. It is always best to select the block that will last you for a few years because you will be able to maintain one publisher prefix, and minimize the unit cost per ISBN. When purchasing a larger block of ISBNs, the price per ISBN decreases.

What is the format of the new ISBN-13?

Every ISBN will consist of thirteen digits in 2007. The thirteen digit number is divided into five parts of variable length, each part separated by a hyphen.

Does the ISBN-13 have any meaning imbedded in the numbers?

The five parts of an ISBN are as follows:

1. The current ISBN-13 will be prefixed by "978"

2. Group or country identifier which identifies a national or geographic grouping of publishers;

3. Publisher identifier which identifies a particular publisher within a group;

4. Title identifier which identifies a particular title or edition of a title;

5. Check digit is the single digit at the end of the ISBN which validates the ISBN.

I want to sell my book on Amazon, how do I get an ISBN for it?

ISBN prefixes are issued to publishers by national ISBN agencies. A list of the agencies is at www.isbn.org

I want to catalog my books using ISBN. How can I use ISBN to get title, author, etc?

If you're interested in cataloging a book collection check out Zarf's bookscanning project http://www.eblong.com/zarf/bookscan/index.html. Any barcode scanner made for the PC can be used to scan these barcodes.

We've found a nice application that helps you use ISBN to get metadata into a personal database. It's called ReaderWare

http://www.sellshareware.com/ProgramInfo.asp?AfID=9583&PrID=39218 .

ReaderWare consists of 3 separate programs for cataloging books, CD's and videos. All feature ReaderWare auto-catalog, the easiest way to catalog your collection. Simply scan or enter the product barcode or ISBN, ReaderWare does the rest. It will search the internet and automatically catalog the item for you, complete with cover art. Can be used with virtually any barcode reader. Other features include table, tree and fish eye views, easy to use wizards, integrated backup and restore, customizable reports, import/export, standalone or client/server mode, SQL database, Palm pilot support.

Where can I get an ISBN database?

If you need an ISBN database, you have the choice of buying one or collecting free data. Because most book data is available for free, there's not a big market for ISBN databases. Nonetheless you can subscribe to books-in-print data services from Library of Congress (recommended), Muse (recommended, but expensive), Baker & Taylor and Ingram. Most people asking this question are interested in free data, which unfortunately means they need to know about "MARC records" and "Z39.50". MARC records are how libraries add book data to their catalogs, and Z39.50 is a protocol (like http) used to request and deliver MARC records. Luckily, you don't need to know much more than that. Endnote, from ISIResearchSoft is software that can connect to libraries using Z39.50 to download book data. You can also use it with MSWord to automate the production of reference lists. You should be able to get all the ISBN data that you need with Endnote. (There's also a version for Mac)

Chapter 4 – Resources

10 for $250 or 1 for $125 – publisher listed is YOU!
http://www.isbn.org/standards/home/index.asp

$55
http://www.isbn-us.com/

Free but you must have a Canadian address
http://www.collectionscanada.gc.ca/ciss-
ssci/app/index.php?&lang=eng

$19.99
http://www.mycheapisbn.com/shop/buy-obtain-isbn-print-or-
ebook/?gclid=CNaVydWz8rQCFe5FMgodnTkAog

$9.99 - Publisher listed is ePubBud and not YOU!
http://epubbud.com/

I Have a Special Gift for My Readers

I appreciate my readers for without them I am just another author attempting to make a difference.

My readers and I have in common a passion for the written word as well as the desire to learn and grow from books.

My special offer to you is a massive ebook library that I have compiled over the years. It contains hundreds of fiction and non-fiction ebooks in Adobe Acrobat PDF format as well as the Greek classics and old literary classics too.

In fact, this library is so massive to completely download the entire library will require over 5 GBs open on your desktop.

Use the link below and scan all of the ebooks in the library. You can select the ebooks you want individually or download the entire library.

The link below does not expire after a given time period so you are free to return for more books rather than clog your desktop. And feel free to give the link to your friends who enjoy reading too.

I thank you for reading my book and hope if you are pleased that you will leave me an honest review so that I can improve my work and or write books that appeal to your interests.

Okay, here is the link…

http://tinyurl.com/special-readers-promo

PS: If you wish to reach me personally for any reason you may simply write to mailto:support@epubwealth.com.

I answer all of my emails so rest assured I will respond.

Meet the Author

Dr. Leland Benton is Director of Applied Web Info, a holding company for ePubWealth.com, a leading ePublisher company based in Utah. With over 21,000 resellers in over 22-countries, ePubWealth.com is a leader in ePublishing, book promotion, and ebook marketing.

As the creator and author of "The ePubWealth Program," Leland teaches up-and-coming authors the ins-and-outs of today's ePublishing world. He has assisted hundreds of authors make it big in the ePublishing world.

Leland also created a series of external book promotion programs and teaches authors how to promote their books using external marketing sources.

Leland is also the Managing Director of Applied Mind Sciences, the company's mind research unit and Chief Forensics Investigator for the company's ForensicsNation unit. He is active in privacy rights through the company's PrivacyNations unit and is an expert in survival planning and disaster relief through the company's SurvivalNations unit.

Leland resides in Southern Utah.

http://www.amazon.com/author/lelandbenton

Visit some of his websites
http://appliedmindsciences.com/
http://appliedwebinfo.com/
http://BoolbuilderPLUS.com
http://embarrassingproblemsfix.com/
http://www.epubwealth.com/
http://forensicsnation.com/
http://neternatives.com/
http://privacynations.com/

http://survivalnations.com/
http://thebentonkitchen.com
http://theolegions.org

Made in the USA
San Bernardino, CA
03 December 2016